Michael Schumacher

Andy Croft

Published in association with The Basic Skills Agency

Hodder & Stoughton
A MEMBER OF THE HODDER HEADLINE GROUP

Acknowledgements
Cover: © Empics
Photos: pp. 4, 7, 9, 12, 17, 19 © Allsport; p. 14 © Jen Little/Empics; p. 22 © Empics; p. 24 © Popperfoto.

Orders: please contact Bookpoint Ltd, 130 Milton Park, Abingdon, Oxon OX14 4SB. Telephone: (44) 01235 827720, Fax: (44) 01235 400454. Lines are open from 9.00 – 6.00, Monday to Saturday, with a 24 hour message answering service. Email address: orders@bookpoint.co.uk

British Library Cataloguing in Publication Data
A catalogue record for this title is available from The British Library

ISBN 0 340 84882 0

First published 2002
Impression number   10 9 8 7 6 5 4 3 2 1
Year   2007 2006 2005 2004 2003 2002

Copyright © 2002 Andy Croft

Typeset by SX Composing DTP, Rayleigh, Essex.
Printed in Great Britain for Hodder & Stoughton Educational, a division of Hodder Headline Plc, 338 Euston Road, London NW1 3BH by The Bath Press Ltd, Bath.

Contents

Introduction

He is fast.

He is brave.

He thinks quickly.

He is cool.

He is calm.

He reacts quickly.

He is confident.

He is very sure of himself.

He knows he is the best.

He has been World Champion three times.

He is one of the greatest drivers
in the history of Formula One.

His name is Michael Schumacher.

1   Go-karts

Michael Schumacher was born
on 3 January 1969
in Kerpen, near Cologne in Germany.
His father Rolf was a builder.

His parents gave Michael
a little pedal go-kart
when he was small.
One day his Dad fitted a motorbike engine to it.
Michael Schumacher started driving
at the age of four!

As he grew older
he liked judo and playing football.
But he liked go-karting best.

When Michael was eleven,
his parents took him to
the World Go-karting Championships.

When Michael was twelve,
his father started work at a local go-kart track.
The family moved there.
Michael could practise on the track
whenever he wanted.
In 1983 the World Go-karting Championships
were held there.
Michael decided to enter.
He was only fifteen,
but he won the German Junior Championship.

The next year he entered
the World Go-karting Championships at Le Mans.
He was only sixteen,
but he was second in the World Juniors.
The following year he won the German Seniors.
He was still only seventeen.
He won it again in 1986.

Michael driving for Jordan at the 1991 Belgian Grand Prix.

2 Benetton

Michael began training as a mechanic.
But people were beginning to notice
the go-kart kid.
He was asked to drive in Formula Koenig.
He won it.
He was asked to drive in German Formula Three.
He came third.
The next year he won it.

In 1991 the Jordan Formula One team
needed a driver in the Belgian Grand Prix.
Their regular driver was in prison.
They asked Michael to drive for them.
He said yes.
He was fourth fastest in the warm-up
and seventh on the grid.

Everyone was very impressed
by the confident twenty-two year-old.
He knew he was ready for Formula One.
Jordan wanted to sign him.
But he joined the Benetton team.

In 1992, he won the Belgian Grand Prix.
He came third in the Drivers' World Championship.
It was his first season in Formula One.

In 1993, he won the Portuguese Grand Prix.
He came fourth in the Drivers'
World Championship.

Michael celebrates after winning the 1992 Belgian
Grand Prix for Benetton.

3 World Champion

Was he good enough to be World Champion?
Michael Schumacher thought so.

Michael started off badly in 1994.
He was banned from four races
because he ignored a flag.
But he went on to win eight
Grand Prix races.

The last race of the season was in Australia.
Damon Hill was only one point
behind Schumacher.
Only he could beat Schumacher
for the world title.
Everything depended on this race.

Schumacher was in the lead.
Damon Hill was close behind him.

On the 36th lap, Schumacher hit a wall.
He made it back on to the track
as Hill tried to overtake him.
Schumacher tried to block him.
Hill tried to squeeze through the gap.
The gap wasn't big enough.
CRASH!

Michael leads Damon Hill at the 1994 Australian Grand Prix, shortly
before their crash.

Both cars were damaged,
so they had to pull out of the race.

Michael Schumacher had done it!
He was World Champion.
He was Germany's first World Champion.

In 1995, he won nine Grand Prix races.
He clashed several times with Hill.
But he won the Drivers' Championship
again for Benetton.
Damon Hill was second again.
At twenty-six, Schumacher was the youngest
double World Champion in history.
Only six other drivers have ever
won it two years running.

Michael drove sixty-nine races for Benetton.
He won nineteen of them.
He was in pole position ten times.
And he won two World Championships.

He was still only twenty-six.

4 Ferarri

By 1996 Schumacher wanted a new challenge.
He joined the Ferrari team.
Lots of famous drivers have driven red Ferraris.
But it was a long time since Ferrari
last won the World Championship.
Schumacher wanted to win it again for Ferrari.
Could he do it?

He won three races in his first year,
in Spain, Belgium and Italy.
But the Ferrari F310 gave him problems.
This time Damon Hill was World Champion.
Schumacher came third.

Rivals: Michael and Damon Hill.

The next year he was driving a better car.
He won five Grand Prix races.
The last race of the season was
the European Grand Prix.
Jacques Villeneuve was only one point
behind Schumacher.
Only he could beat Schumacher
for the world title.
Everything depended on this race.

Half-way through the race
Schumacher had problems with his car.
Villeneuve tried to pass him on the inside.
Schumacher tried to block him
but he ended up in the gravel.
Villeneuve finished the race
and won the World Championship.
Schumacher was stripped of second place
for dangerous driving.

Michael at pole position on the starting grid.

Ninetenn ninety-eight began badly
for Michael Schumacher.
His engine broke down.
He was penalised for forcing
another car off the track.
He was penalised for missing a flag.
But he still won six Grand Prix races.
He was only four points behind Mika Hakkinen.

Everything depended on
the last race of the season in Japan.
Schumacher was in pole position
but he stalled on the grid.
He had to start at the back.
He battled back to third place.
But on lap thirty-one he had a puncture.
Hakkinen won the race.
And the title.
Schumacher came second.

Nineteen ninety-nine started well.
Michael won at Monaco and San Marino.
Then things started going wrong.
He almost won in Brazil,
despite a broken wing and a puncture.
He was leading in the Canadian Grand Prix
until he crashed into the wall.
He was still in second place behind Hakkinen.
But then he came off the track at high speed
in the British Grand Prix.
He broke both bones in his right leg
and missed the next six races.
He was back for the last two races of the season.
He came second in both.
But it was too late.
Hakkinen won the title again.
Schumacher was fifth.

People were starting to say
Schumacher would never win the title for Ferrari.

Michael's car being taken away after his crash at Silverstone in 1999.

5 Danger

Formula One is a very dangerous sport.
Many famous drivers have died on the track,
such as Gilles Villeneuve
and Schumacher's hero Ayrton Senna.

But Michael Schumacher likes danger.
He likes risk.
He likes driving in the wet.
He even likes driving on ice.
He has hit a wall.
He has hit a barrier.
His car has caught fire.
His car has been thrown into the air.
He has been hit by other cars.

One of his closest rivals is his younger brother Ralf.

But nothing can stop
Michael Schumacher.
That's why he is the best.

Michael's hero, Ayrton Senna (right), celebrates his World
Championship win in 1991. He died on the track in 1994.

6   World Champion Again

In 2000, Schumacher had a new car,
the F1-2000.
He won the first three Grand Prix races,
in Australia, Brazil and San Marino.

Mika Hakkinen and David Coulthard
were both chasing Schumacher for the title.
But he couldn't stop winning.
He won in Europe and Canada.
He won in Italy and the USA.
He only had to win in Japan to be World Champion.
He beat Hakkinen by 1.84 seconds.

Michael Schumacher was World Champion
for the third time.
After twenty-one years, Ferrari had
a World Champion at last.
There was still one more race left.
Schumacher didn't need to win it.
But he did anyway.

7   **And Again**

Could Michael Schumacher
be World Champion four times?
Only two drivers had ever done this before.
Could he do it?

In 2001 he won in:
Australia,
Malaysia,
Spain,
Monaco,
Europe
and France.
He came second in:
Brazil,
Austria,
Canada
and Britain.

Michael celebrates winning the World Championship
in 2001.

Then came the Hungarian Grand Prix.
All he had to do was win this race
to win the World Championship.
Could he do it?
He drove at an average speed of 112 miles an hour.
He won the race.
It was his 51st Grand Prix win.
It equalled Alain Prost's record.

There were still four races to go.
But no-one could catch him.
He won two of them.
He had twice as many points
as his nearest rival,
David Coulthard.

Michael Schumacher was World Champion again.
For the fourth time.

8 The Man Behind the Wheel

His fans call him 'Schumi' or 'Schuey'.
He is the highest-paid sportsperson in the world.
He earns thirty million dollars a year from racing.
He earns even more
from sponsorship and advertising.

But he is still a family man.
He enjoys being at his houses
in Switzerland and Norway.
He enjoys being with his wife Corinna,
their children Gina-Maria and Mick,
and their dogs Mosley and Ecclestone.

His favourite food is ice-cream.
He likes swimming and skiing.
He likes playing tennis and football.
He even plays football for his
local team in Switzerland.
He has lots of cars and a motorbike.
He still likes go-karting.

Michael plays football in his spare time. Here he is playing
a match for charity in 2001.

His fans adore him.
There is even a pizza named after him!
Fans stop him everywhere for autographs.
Once he was having his hair cut.
By the time the barber finished
there were over fifty fans outside the shop.
A fan once jumped out in front of his car
and Michael Schumacher ran him over.

Michael Schumacher is one of the greatest
Formula One drivers of all time.
But he still wants to win.
He still wants to be the best.

Do you think he can win the title five times?

Michael Schumacher Quiz

1   When was Michael born?

2   How old was he when he started driving?

3   Which racing driver used to be his hero?

4   When did he win his first Grand Prix race?

5   When did he win his first World Championship?

6   What is the name of his current
Formula One team?

7   How many times has he been World Champion?

8   What is his nick-name?